Day and Night

Words by David Bennett
Pictures by Rosalinda Kightley

A BANTAM LITTLE ROOSTER BOOK
TM

Toronto · New York · London · Sydney · Auckland

During the day, the sun is in the sky. The sun gives our world light and warmth.

At night, after the sun has set, it is dark.
You may see the moon shining and the
stars twinkling in the sky.

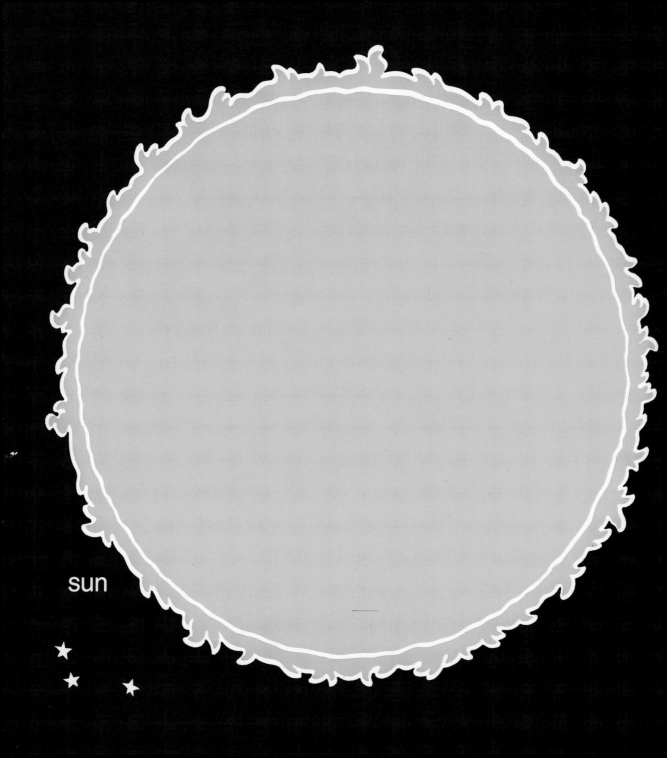

sun

Our world is a planet called Earth.
It floats in space with other planets and
the sun and the moon. The sun is much
bigger than the earth. The moon is
much smaller.

earth

moon

B1

The sun is one of the millions of stars in the sky. It looks bigger than other stars because it is closer to us. Most stars can only be seen at night.

When we see the moon at night, it looks quiet and calm. There is no life on the moon because there is no air to breathe or water to drink.

The earth turns around and around —
it never stops. It takes a whole day and
night for it to go around one time.
When your part of the earth turns to
face the sun, it is daytime.

On the other side of the earth it is nighttime.
The people who live there are going to sleep
when you are waking up in the morning.

Sunrise means the beginning of a new day.

The sun seems to be moving into the sky.

But it isn't — it only looks that way

because the earth is turning.

By the middle of the day, the sun looks as though it has moved high into the sky.
This is the hottest and brightest time of day.
We call it noon.

In some places it gets so hot that people and animals have to stay out of the sun. This is a good time to have lunch.

During the time of day we call afternoon,
your part of the earth begins to turn away
from the sun. The sun looks lower in the sky.
The sky is not as bright, and the air is cooler.

At the end of the day, your part of the earth turns farther away from the sun. Day turns into evening.

At sunset, the sun disappears from view,
and the sky changes color — sometimes
it turns orange and red and even pink.

Without light and warmth from the sun, it becomes dark and cool outside. It is nighttime. Your part of the earth has turned away from the sun.

We can make our own
light and warmth.
Do you know how?

Even though you cannot see the sun at night, its light still reaches the moon and other parts of the earth.

The sun's light makes the moon shine in the sky. Stars make their own light. But the moon has no light of its own.

Sometimes the moon seems to change its shape. Even though we can only see part of the moon on some nights, the whole moon is always there.

At night, it is time to go to sleep. But some animals, such as bats and owls, are wide-awake. They sleep during the day.

During the night, the earth keeps turning.

Soon your part of the world is facing the sun again. As the sun appears in the sky, a new day begins.

Do you know what is happening on the other side of the earth?

BEAR REVIEW

1. The earth is always turning. The sun does not move.

2. When your part of the earth is facing the sun, it is daytime.

3. When your part of the earth turns away from the sun, it is nighttime.

4. The people who live on the other side of the earth are going to sleep when you are waking up in the morning.